THE FRUGAL MINDSET

"Mastering Money, Living Richly: Unleashing the Power of The Frugal Mindset"

VINCENT CLARK

Copyright ©

Dedication

In heartfelt dedication to those who dare to challenge conventional notions of wealth and abundance, who understand that true richness lies not in material possessions but in the wisdom of mindful living. To the frugal pioneers, the visionaries of financial freedom, who courageously embrace simplicity and resourcefulness on their journey towards prosperity. This dedication is for the seekers of sustainable wealth, the guardians of future generations, and the stewards of our planet's well-being. May your commitment to the frugal mindset inspire others to cultivate conscious consumption, prioritize value over excess, and discover the profound joy of living with purpose and intention.

Table of Contents

Acknowledgments

I extend my deepest gratitude to all those whose support and guidance have illuminated the path of this endeavor. To my family, whose unwavering encouragement and understanding sustained me through countless hours of writing and reflection. To my friends, whose belief in my vision bolstered my resolve and fueled my creativity. To the mentors and advisors whose wisdom and insight shaped the direction of this work. To the readers, whose curiosity and open-mindedness make sharing these ideas possible. Your contributions, whether large or small, have enriched this journey beyond measure, and for that, I am profoundly thankful.

Preface

In the fast-paced world of consumerism and materialism, the concept of frugality often stands in stark contrast, challenging the prevailing norms of excess and instant gratification. This book, "The Frugal Mindset," is born out of a deep conviction that true wealth lies not in the accumulation of possessions, but in the cultivation of a mindful approach to living.

In the preface of this book, I invite you to embark on a transformative journey—one that transcends mere financial considerations and delves into the profound philosophy of frugality. Here, we explore the art of intentional living, where every decision is guided by a commitment to value, sustainability, and purpose.

Through the pages that follow, we will uncover the principles of frugal living, from budgeting basics to wealth-building strategies, from mindful spending habits to resourcefulness and DIY culture. We will examine the intersection of frugality with sustainability and social impact, and discover how adopting a frugal mindset can not only improve our finances but also contribute to a more equitable and sustainable world.

As we embark on this journey together, I encourage you to approach these ideas with an open mind and a willingness to challenge conventional wisdom. May "The Frugal Mindset" serve as a beacon of inspiration and empowerment, guiding you toward a life of abundance, fulfillment, and financial freedom.

Chapter 1.

Understanding Frugality

- Exploring the Concept of Frugality

In the opening chapter, "Understanding Frugality," we embark on a journey to explore the multifaceted concept of frugality. We delve into its roots, examining its historical significance and evolution over time. From its humble beginnings as a virtue extolled by ancient philosophers to its modern-day interpretation as a savvy financial strategy, we uncover the various dimensions of frugality.

Through insightful anecdotes and practical examples, we dissect the essence of frugal living, distinguishing it from mere penny-pinching or deprivation. Frugality, as we come to understand, is not about sacrificing quality of life but rather about making intentional choices that align with our values and long-term goals.

We challenge common misconceptions surrounding frugality, debunking the notion that it entails a life of austerity or self-denial. Instead, we highlight the liberating power of frugality, demonstrating how it can foster creativity, resourcefulness, and a deeper sense of satisfaction.

By the end of this chapter, readers will have gained a comprehensive understanding of frugality as more than just a financial strategy—it is a mindset, a philosophy, and a pathway to greater financial freedom and fulfillment.

– Benefits of Adopting a Frugal Mindset

In this chapter, we explore the numerous benefits of adopting a frugal mindset, demonstrating how it can positively impact every aspect of our lives. We delve into the tangible and intangible rewards that come from embracing frugality, from financial stability to enhanced well-being.

First and foremost, we uncover how a frugal mindset empowers individuals to take control of their finances, allowing them to live within their means, reduce debt, and build sustainable wealth over time. By prioritizing needs over wants and practicing mindful spending habits, individuals can achieve greater financial security and freedom.

Beyond the realm of finances, we examine how frugality fosters a sense of resourcefulness and creativity, encouraging individuals to find innovative solutions to everyday challenges. By learning to make the most of what they have, people can live more sustainably and reduce their environmental impact.

Moreover, we explore the psychological benefits of frugality, such as reduced stress and increased happiness. By shifting focus away from material possessions and towards experiences and relationships, individuals can cultivate a deeper sense of fulfillment and contentment in their lives.

Ultimately, this chapter serves as a compelling testament to the transformative power of a frugal mindset. By embracing frugality, individuals can not only improve their financial well-being but also enhance their overall quality of life, leading to greater happiness, resilience, and fulfillment.

- Overcoming Misconceptions About Frugality

In this chapter, we confront common misconceptions surrounding frugality, shedding light on the truth behind the stereotypes and misunderstandings that often accompany this mindset. We aim to dispel myths and misconceptions, allowing readers to develop a more nuanced understanding of what it truly means to embrace frugality.

One prevalent misconception we address is the belief that frugality equates to deprivation or a lower quality of life. Through real-life examples and evidence-based research, we demonstrate that frugality is not about sacrificing enjoyment or comfort but rather about making intentional choices that align with one's values and priorities.

Another misconception we tackle is the idea that frugality is only for those on a tight budget or facing financial hardship. We show that frugality is a mindset that can benefit individuals across all income levels, from those seeking to save money to those aiming to live more sustainably or pursue their long-term goals.

Additionally, we address the misconception that frugality requires extreme measures or a radical lifestyle change. By offering practical tips and strategies for incorporating frugality into everyday life, we illustrate how small, incremental changes can lead to significant savings and improvements in financial well-being.

Overall, this chapter serves as a guide for readers to overcome common misconceptions about frugality and embrace it as a powerful tool for achieving financial freedom, sustainability, and fulfillment. By challenging preconceived notions and exploring the true essence of frugality, readers can unlock the transformative potential of this mindset in their own lives.

Chapter 2.

Principles of Frugal Living

- Setting Financial Goals

Setting financial goals is a fundamental aspect of adopting a frugal lifestyle. It serves as a guiding light, directing our actions and decisions toward achieving financial stability, security, and ultimately, freedom. In this chapter, we explore the principles of setting financial goals within the context of frugal living and provide practical strategies for success.

1. Define Your Objectives: The first step in setting financial goals is to clearly define what you want to achieve. Take the time to reflect on your values, aspirations, and

priorities. Are you looking to pay off debt, save for a major purchase, or invest for retirement? By understanding your objectives, you can tailor your financial goals to align with your circumstances and desires.

2. Be Specific and Measurable: When setting financial goals, it's essential to be specific and measurable. Rather than setting vague goals like "save money" or "pay off debt," break them down into concrete targets. For example, aim to save $5,000 for an emergency fund or pay off $10,000 of credit card debt within a year. This specificity allows you to track your progress and stay motivated along the way.

3. Prioritize Your Goals: Not all financial goals are created equal. Some may be more urgent or important than others.

Prioritize your goals based on factors such as their impact on your financial well-being, timeline, and feasibility. Start with high-priority goals that address immediate needs or offer significant long-term benefits, then work your way down the list.

4. Make Goals Achievable: While it's important to dream big, it's equally crucial to set realistic and achievable goals. Be honest with yourself about your financial situation and capabilities. Set goals that stretch you out of your comfort zone but are still within reach with dedication and effort. Breaking larger goals into smaller, manageable steps can make them feel more attainable and keep you motivated along the way.

5. Set Timeframes: Time is a valuable resource when it comes to achieving

financial goals. Without clear deadlines, goals can linger indefinitely, losing momentum and focus. Set specific timeframes for achieving each goal, whether it's weeks, months, or years. This sense of urgency can help you stay disciplined and focused on taking consistent action toward your objectives.

6. Review and Adjust Regularly: Financial goals are not set in stone. Life circumstances change, priorities shift, and unexpected challenges arise. Regularly review your goals to ensure they remain relevant and aligned with your current situation and aspirations. Be flexible and willing to adjust your goals as needed, taking into account new opportunities, setbacks, or changes in priorities.

By adhering to these principles of setting financial goals, you can lay a solid foundation for frugal living and financial success. Remember that the journey toward achieving your goals may not always be smooth, but with determination, perseverance, and a clear vision, you can turn your financial aspirations into reality.

- Budgeting Basics: Making Every Dollar Count

Budgeting lies at the heart of frugal living, serving as a powerful tool for managing finances effectively and maximizing resources. In this section, we delve into the fundamental principles of budgeting and offer practical tips for making every dollar count.

1. Track Your Expenses: The first step in creating an effective budget is to understand where your money is going. Keep track of all your expenses, from fixed costs like rent and utilities to variable expenses like groceries and entertainment. This can be done through apps, spreadsheets, or simply pen and paper. By gaining insight into your spending habits, you can identify areas where you may be overspending and make necessary adjustments.

2. Set Financial Goals: Budgeting is not just about tracking expenses; it's also about aligning your spending with your financial goals. Identify your short-term and long-term objectives, whether it's saving for a vacation, paying off debt, or

building an emergency fund. Allocate a portion of your budget towards these goals, prioritizing them over non-essential expenses.

3. Create a Realistic Budget: Based on your income and expenses, create a realistic budget that reflects your financial priorities and constraints. Allocate funds for essential expenses such as housing, transportation, groceries, and utilities first, then allocate the remaining funds towards savings, debt repayment, and discretionary spending. Be sure to leave room for unexpected expenses and emergencies by building a buffer in your budget.

4. Monitor and Adjust: Budgeting is an ongoing process that requires regular monitoring and adjustment. Track your spending regularly to ensure you are

staying within your budgeted limits. If you find yourself consistently overspending in certain areas, reassess your budget and make necessary adjustments. Look for opportunities to cut back on non-essential expenses and redirect those funds toward your financial goals.

5. Embrace Frugal Habits: Frugal living is all about maximizing value and minimizing waste. Look for ways to trim expenses without sacrificing the quality of life. This could involve shopping sales, buying in bulk, cooking at home, using coupons, or finding free or low-cost entertainment options. Small changes in spending habits can add up to significant savings over time.

6. Plan for the Future: In addition to managing day-to-day expenses, budgeting also involves planning for the

future. Allocate funds towards savings and investments to build financial security and achieve long-term goals such as retirement. Consider automating savings contributions to ensure they are prioritized consistently.

By mastering the basics of budgeting and adopting frugal habits, you can take control of your finances, make every dollar count, and work towards achieving your financial goals. Remember that budgeting is a journey, and success comes from consistency, discipline, and a willingness to adapt to changing circumstances.

- Strategies for Cutting Expenses Without Sacrificing Quality of Life

Living frugally doesn't mean sacrificing your quality of life; it's about making intentional choices to maximize value and minimize waste. In this section, we explore practical strategies for reducing expenses without compromising on the things that matter most.

1. Evaluate Your Needs vs. Wants: Start by distinguishing between essential needs and discretionary wants. Focus your spending on fulfilling your needs, such as housing, food, transportation, and healthcare, while minimizing expenditures on non-essential items and indulgences.

2. Shop Smart: Take a strategic approach to shopping by comparing prices, seeking out sales and discounts, and using coupons or promo codes. Consider buying generic brands instead of name brands, as they often offer similar quality at a lower cost. Additionally, buy in bulk for items you frequently use to save money over time.

3. Reduce Fixed Expenses: Look for opportunities to trim fixed expenses, such as housing, utilities, and subscriptions. Consider downsizing to a smaller living space, negotiating lower interest rates on loans and credit cards, or canceling unused or unnecessary subscriptions and memberships.

4. Cut Discretionary Spending: Identify areas where you can cut back on

discretionary spending without significantly impacting your quality of life. This could involve dining out less frequently, limiting impulse purchases, or finding free or low-cost alternatives to expensive hobbies and entertainment.

5. Embrace DIY: Save money by taking a do-it-yourself approach to tasks and projects whenever possible. Whether it's cooking meals at home, repairing items instead of replacing them, or tackling home improvement projects yourself, embracing a DIY mindset can lead to significant savings over time.

6. Practice Minimalism: Adopting a minimalist lifestyle can help you declutter your belongings and simplify your life, leading to reduced expenses and increased satisfaction. Focus on owning fewer possessions that serve a purpose

and bring you joy, rather than accumulating unnecessary clutter.

7. Negotiate and Bargain: Don't be afraid to negotiate prices or ask for discounts when making purchases, especially for big-ticket items or services. Many retailers and service providers are willing to negotiate to secure your business, so it never hurts to ask for a better deal.

8. Prioritize Quality Over Quantity: Invest in high-quality, durable items that are built to last, even if they come with a higher upfront cost. While it may seem counterintuitive, opting for quality over quantity can save you money in the long run by reducing the need for frequent replacements and repairs.

By implementing these strategies, you can effectively cut expenses without sacrificing your quality of life. Remember that frugality is about making intentional choices that align with your values and priorities, allowing you to live a fulfilling life while also achieving financial security and freedom.

Chapter 3.

Mindful Spending Habits

- Identifying Wants vs. Needs

Practicing mindfulness in spending involves understanding the distinction between wants and needs. In this section, we delve into the importance of discerning between the two and offer strategies for making intentional spending decisions.

1. Define Wants and Needs: Start by clarifying what constitutes a want versus a need. Needs are essential for survival

and basic well-being, such as food, shelter, clothing, and healthcare. Wants, on the other hand, are desires or preferences that enhance our quality of life but are not necessary for survival.

2. Prioritize Needs: When creating a budget or making purchasing decisions, prioritize meeting your needs first. Allocate funds towards essential expenses such as housing, utilities, groceries, and healthcare before considering discretionary spending on wants.

3. Question Your Motives: Before making a purchase, pause and reflect on your motives behind it. Are you buying out of necessity, or is it driven by impulse or societal pressure? Taking a moment to examine your intentions can help you make more mindful and deliberate spending choices.

4. Practice Delayed Gratification: Resist the urge to indulge in impulse purchases by practicing delayed gratification. Instead of making spur-of-the-moment decisions, give yourself time to consider whether the item is a genuine need or merely a fleeting want. If it's a want, consider waiting a designated period, such as 24 hours or a week, before revisiting the decision.

5. Set Spending Limits: Establish clear spending limits for different categories of expenses, particularly discretionary ones. By setting boundaries on how much you're willing to spend on non-essential items, you can avoid overspending and ensure that your financial resources are allocated towards meeting your needs first.

6. Differentiate Between Short-term Pleasure and Long-term Fulfillment: Recognize that while wants may provide immediate gratification, they often pale in comparison to the lasting fulfillment that comes from meeting genuine needs and pursuing meaningful experiences. Prioritize spending on activities, relationships, and pursuits that contribute to your long-term happiness and well-being.

7. Cultivate Gratitude: Develop a mindset of gratitude for what you already have, rather than constantly seeking more. Take stock of the abundance in your life and appreciate the simple pleasures that don't require spending money. Cultivating gratitude can help shift your focus away from material possessions and toward the things that truly matter.

By honing your ability to differentiate between wants and needs, you can cultivate mindful spending habits that align with your values and goals. By prioritizing needs over wants and practicing intentional consumption, you can achieve greater financial stability, reduce unnecessary clutter and waste, and enhance your overall well-being.

– Practicing Delayed Gratification

Delayed gratification is a powerful tool for building self-discipline and achieving long-term goals. In this section, we explore the importance of delaying immediate rewards in favor of greater future benefits and offer practical strategies for incorporating delayed gratification into your life.

1. Understanding Delayed Gratification: Delayed gratification involves resisting the temptation of immediate pleasure or satisfaction to reap greater rewards in the future. It requires the ability to tolerate discomfort or uncertainty in the present for the sake of achieving more significant goals or outcomes down the line.

2. Setting Long-Term Goals: Begin by identifying your long-term goals and aspirations. Whether it's saving for retirement, pursuing higher education, or starting a business, having a clear vision of what you want to achieve motivates you to delay gratification in pursuit of those goals.

3. Breaking Goals into Milestones: Break down your long-term goals into smaller, manageable milestones or objectives. By focusing on making progress towards these smaller goals, you can experience a sense of accomplishment and satisfaction along the way, motivating you to continue delaying gratification.

4. Creating Accountability: Hold yourself accountable for sticking to your goals and delaying gratification by sharing your aspirations with others. This could involve enlisting the support of friends, family members, or mentors who can provide encouragement, accountability, and guidance along your journey.

5. Practicing Self-Control: Develop strategies for managing impulses and urges that threaten to derail your

progress toward your goals. This could involve techniques such as mindfulness meditation, distraction techniques, or simply taking a step back and reflecting on the long-term consequences of giving in to immediate gratification.

6. Rewarding Progress: Acknowledge and reward yourself for making progress towards your goals, even if it's just small steps forward. Celebrate milestones and achievements along the way to reinforce the value of delayed gratification and motivate continued effort and perseverance.

7. Cultivating Patience: Recognize that delayed gratification requires patience and perseverance. It's not always easy to resist immediate rewards, especially in a society that encourages instant gratification. Cultivate patience by

practicing mindfulness, embracing uncertainty, and focusing on the long-term benefits of delaying gratification.

By incorporating these strategies into your life, you can harness the power of delayed gratification to achieve your long-term goals, build self-discipline, and ultimately lead a more fulfilling and purposeful life. Remember that delayed gratification is a skill that can be cultivated over time with practice and dedication, and the rewards of patience and perseverance are well worth the effort.

- Mindfulness Techniques for Curbing Impulse Purchases

Impulse purchases can derail even the most carefully crafted budget and financial plan. In this section, we explore mindfulness techniques to help you become more aware of your spending habits and resist the urge to make impulsive purchases.

1. Pause and Reflect: Before making a purchase, take a moment to pause and reflect on your decision. Ask yourself why you want to buy the item and whether it aligns with your values, goals, and budget. Simply taking a few deep breaths can help calm your mind and create space for more deliberate decision-making.

2. Practice the 24-Hour Rule: Implement the 24-hour rule, which involves waiting a designated period, such as 24 hours, before making non-essential purchases. Use this time to consider whether the item is a genuine need or merely a passing desire. Often, you'll find that the impulse to buy fades with time, allowing you to make a more rational decision.

3. Create a Shopping List: Before heading to the store or browsing online, create a shopping list of items you genuinely need or have planned to purchase. Stick to your list and avoid deviating from it unless necessary. This helps prevent impulse buys triggered by attractive displays or marketing tactics.

4. Set Spending Limits: Establish clear spending limits for discretionary

purchases and stick to them. Determine how much you're willing to spend on non-essential items each month and allocate funds accordingly. Having a predefined budget helps curb impulse spending and encourages more mindful consumption.

5. Identify Triggers: Become aware of the situations, emotions, or triggers that tend to lead to impulse purchases. Whether it's boredom, stress, or social pressure, understanding your triggers allows you to develop strategies for managing them more effectively. Find alternative ways to address underlying needs or emotions, such as going for a walk, practicing mindfulness, or engaging in a hobby.

6. Visualize the Opportunity Cost: Consider the opportunity cost of making an impulse purchase—the value of what

you could have done with the money instead. Visualize how the money could be allocated towards achieving your financial goals, such as paying off debt, saving for a vacation, or investing for the future. This perspective shift can help you prioritize your spending and resist the lure of impulse buys.

7. Practice Gratitude: Cultivate a mindset of gratitude for what you already have rather than constantly seeking more. Take stock of the abundance in your life and appreciate the things that bring you joy and fulfillment without requiring additional purchases. Focusing on gratitude can help reduce the desire for unnecessary possessions and foster contentment with what you have.

By incorporating these mindfulness techniques into your daily life, you can become more conscious of your spending habits, resist impulse purchases, and make more intentional choices that align with your financial goals and values. Mindfulness empowers you to take control of your finances and live a more purposeful and fulfilling life.

Chapter4.

Resourcefulness and DIY Culture

- Embracing DIY Projects for Savings

In this section, we explore the value of resourcefulness and the benefits of embracing do-it-yourself (DIY) projects as a means of saving money and maximizing resources.

1. Utilizing Existing Skills and Talents: Start by identifying your existing skills and talents that can be leveraged for DIY projects. Whether it's woodworking, sewing, cooking, gardening, or home

repairs, tap into your abilities to tackle tasks and projects on your own rather than outsourcing them to professionals.

2. Learning New Skills: Embrace a mindset of lifelong learning by acquiring new skills and knowledge through DIY projects. With the abundance of online tutorials, courses, and resources available, it's easier than ever to learn how to do things yourself. From basic home repairs to complex crafts, there's a wealth of information at your fingertips waiting to be explored.

3. Saving Money on Goods and Services: DIY projects offer significant cost savings compared to purchasing goods or hiring professionals for services. Whether it's refurbishing furniture, making homemade cleaning products, or growing your vegetables, DIY allows you to produce

high-quality items at a fraction of the cost of buying them pre-made or hiring someone else to do it for you.

4. Customization and Personalization: One of the greatest benefits of DIY projects is the ability to customize and personalize items to suit your preferences and tastes. Whether it's crafting handmade gifts, designing your clothing, or building custom furniture, DIY allows you to create unique and one-of-a-kind pieces that reflect your individuality.

5. Reducing Waste and Environmental Impact: By repurposing materials and resources and avoiding unnecessary consumption, DIY projects contribute to reducing waste and minimizing environmental impact. Instead of discarding old items or purchasing new ones, consider how they can be

transformed or repurposed through creative DIY techniques.

6. Fostering Creativity and Innovation: Engaging in DIY projects fosters creativity and innovation by encouraging experimentation, problem-solving, and out-of-the-box thinking. It provides an opportunity to explore new ideas, express yourself artistically, and push the boundaries of what's possible.

7. Building Confidence and Self-Reliance: Finally, DIY projects help build confidence and self-reliance by empowering you to take control of your surroundings and tackle challenges independently. With each successful project completed, you gain a sense of accomplishment and mastery that boosts your self-esteem and resilience.

By embracing resourcefulness and DIY culture, you can unlock a world of opportunities for savings, creativity, and self-expression. Whether you're refurbishing old furniture, planting a garden, or learning how to fix a leaky faucet, DIY projects offer countless benefits that extend far beyond the realm of cost savings. Embrace the challenge, unleash your creativity, and discover the satisfaction of doing it yourself.

- Repurposing and Upcycling: Making the Most of What You Have

In this section, we explore the art of repurposing and upcycling as creative ways to breathe new life into old or unused items, reducing waste, and maximizing resources.

1. Reimagining Possibilities: Repurposing and upcycling involve reimagining the potential of everyday objects beyond their original purpose. Instead of discarding items that are no longer needed or functional, consider how they can be transformed or repurposed into something new and useful.

2. Creative Problem-Solving: Engage your creativity and problem-solving skills to find innovative ways to repurpose items. Whether it's turning old clothing into reusable shopping bags, transforming pallets into furniture, or repurposing mason jars into storage containers, the possibilities are endless when you think outside the box.

3. Reducing Waste: Repurposing and upcycling help reduce waste by giving new life to items that would otherwise end up in landfills. By extending the lifespan of products and materials, you contribute to a more sustainable and environmentally friendly way of living.

4. Saving Money: One of the most significant benefits of repurposing and upcycling is the cost savings it offers. Instead of purchasing new items, you can

often repurpose existing ones for little to no cost, saving money while reducing consumption and waste.

5. Personalization and Customization: Repurposing and upcycling allow you to personalize and customize items to suit your tastes and preferences. Whether it's painting, embellishing, or redesigning, you can put your unique stamp on repurposed creations, making them truly one-of-a-kind.

6. Learning New Skills: Engaging in repurposing and upcycling projects provides an opportunity to learn new skills and techniques. Whether it's woodworking, sewing, painting, or DIY crafting, each project offers a chance to expand your knowledge and abilities in a hands-on, practical way.

7.   Fostering   Creativity   and Resourcefulness: Repurposing   and upcycling   encourage   creativity, resourcefulness, and a mindset of making do with what you have. Instead of always seeking out new items or solutions, you learn to work with the materials and resources you already possess, fostering a sense of ingenuity and self-reliance.

By embracing the principles of repurposing and upcycling, you can not only reduce waste and save money but also unleash your creativity, learn new skills, and contribute to a more sustainable way of living. Whether you're repurposing old furniture, upcycling clothing, or finding new uses for household items, every act of creativity and resourcefulness brings us one step closer to a more resilient and mindful lifestyle.

- Cultivating a Resourceful Mindset in Everyday Life

In this section, we explore practical strategies for fostering a resourceful mindset—a way of thinking that emphasizes creativity, adaptability, and making the most of available resources—in various aspects of daily life.

1. Embrace Creativity: Cultivate a mindset of creativity by approaching challenges and problems with an open mind and a willingness to explore unconventional solutions. Instead of seeing limitations, see opportunities for innovation and ingenuity.

2. Practice Adaptability: Develop the ability to adapt to changing

circumstances and unexpected challenges. Instead of being deterred by setbacks or obstacles, view them as opportunities to learn, grow, and find creative solutions.

3. Be Curious and Inquisitive: Cultivate a sense of curiosity and inquisitiveness about the world around you. Ask questions, seek out new information, and explore different perspectives. The more curious you are, the more likely you are to discover innovative solutions and opportunities.

4. Foster Problem-Solving Skills: Develop strong problem-solving skills by breaking down complex problems into smaller, more manageable components. Consider multiple perspectives and approaches, and be willing to experiment and iterate until you find a solution that works.

5. Develop a Can-Do Attitude: Cultivate a positive, can-do attitude that empowers you to take on challenges with confidence and resilience. Instead of focusing on what you lack, focus on what you can do with the resources and abilities you have at your disposal.

6. Practice Gratitude: Cultivate a sense of gratitude for the resources and opportunities you have in your life. By appreciating what you have, you can better leverage your resources and make the most of them.

7. Seek Out Learning Opportunities: Continuously seek out opportunities to learn and acquire new skills. Whether it's through formal education, online courses, workshops, or self-directed learning, investing in your personal and

professional development expands your knowledge base and enhances your resourcefulness.

8. Build a Support Network: Surround yourself with supportive individuals who share your values and mindset. Collaborate, share ideas, and draw inspiration from others who embody resourcefulness and creativity in their own lives.

9. Practice Sustainability: Consider the long-term impact of your actions and decisions on the environment and future generations. Embrace sustainable practices and behaviors that minimize waste, conserve resources, and promote resilience and stewardship of the planet.

By incorporating these strategies into your daily life, you can cultivate a resourceful mindset that empowers you to navigate challenges, seize opportunities, and make the most of the resources available to you. Whether you're facing personal, professional, or societal challenges, a resourceful mindset equips you with the tools and mindset needed to thrive in an ever-changing world.

Chapter 5.

Building Wealth Through Frugality

- Investing Wisely: Making Your Money Work for You

Building wealth through frugality is a time-tested strategy that prioritizes mindful spending, disciplined saving, and prudent investing. At its core, frugality involves making deliberate choices to optimize resources and minimize wasteful expenditure. By embracing a frugal lifestyle, individuals can cultivate financial independence and long-term prosperity.

One fundamental aspect of building wealth through frugality is budgeting. Creating a detailed budget allows individuals to track their expenses, identify areas for potential savings, and allocate funds towards their financial goals. By scrutinizing every expenditure, individuals can distinguish between needs and wants, thereby curbing unnecessary spending habits.

Moreover, frugality encourages the adoption of cost-saving measures in everyday life. This may include strategies such as meal planning, purchasing items in bulk, utilizing coupons, and embracing DIY projects. By leveraging these practices, individuals can stretch their dollars further and increase their savings rate, thereby accelerating their journey towards financial freedom.

Another critical component of building wealth through frugality is prioritizing savings. By consistently setting aside a portion of their income, individuals can establish emergency funds, retirement accounts, and investment portfolios. This financial cushion provides a safety net in times of uncertainty and serves as a foundation for future wealth accumulation.

However, perhaps the most impactful aspect of frugality is investing wisely. Instead of squandering resources on frivolous purchases, individuals can redirect their funds towards income-generating assets with the potential for long-term growth. This may include investing in stocks, bonds, mutual funds, real estate, or starting a small business. By harnessing the power of compounding returns, individuals can make their money work for them and exponentially increase their wealth over time.

In essence, building wealth through frugality involves a holistic approach to personal finance, encompassing mindful spending, diligent saving, and strategic investing. By embracing frugality as a guiding principle, individuals can pave the way towards financial security, independence, and ultimately, prosperity.

– Frugal Living and Sustainable Wealth Accumulation

Frugal living is not just about saving money; it's also about cultivating sustainable wealth accumulation practices. By embracing a frugal lifestyle, individuals can achieve financial stability and long-term prosperity while minimizing their environmental impact.

One of the key aspects of frugal living is mindful consumption. Instead of succumbing to the constant urge to buy more, frugal individuals carefully consider their purchases, opting for quality over quantity and prioritizing items that add genuine value to their lives. This mindset not only saves money in the short term but also reduces waste and promotes sustainability by minimizing unnecessary consumption.

Frugal living also encourages resourcefulness and self-sufficiency. Rather than relying solely on external goods and services, frugal individuals seek creative solutions and DIY approaches to meet their needs. Whether it's growing their own food, repairing items instead of replacing them, or finding alternative methods for transportation, frugality fosters a sense of empowerment and resilience in the face of challenges.

Moreover, frugal living goes hand in hand with minimalism, emphasizing the importance of decluttering and simplifying one's life. By eliminating excess possessions and focusing on the essentials, individuals can free up valuable time, space, and mental energy to pursue their passions and goals. This minimalist mindset not only reduces financial clutter but also fosters a sense of clarity and purpose.

When it comes to wealth accumulation, frugal living provides a solid foundation for long-term financial success. By living below their means and prioritizing savings and investment, frugal individuals can build wealth steadily over time. This sustainable approach to wealth accumulation ensures financial security and stability, allowing individuals to weather economic downturns and unexpected expenses with confidence.

In essence, frugal living is not just a means to save money; it's a lifestyle that promotes sustainable wealth accumulation, environmental consciousness, and personal fulfillment. By embracing frugality, individuals can achieve financial independence while also contributing to a more sustainable and equitable world for future generations.

- Strategies for Debt Reduction and Financial Independence

Strategies for debt reduction and achieving financial independence are essential components of personal finance management. By implementing effective tactics, individuals can regain control of their finances, eliminate debt, and pave the way towards financial freedom.

1. Create a Budget: Establishing a comprehensive budget is the first step towards debt reduction and financial independence. By tracking income and expenses, individuals can identify areas where they can cut back and allocate more funds towards debt repayment and savings.

2. Prioritize High-Interest Debt: Focus on paying off high-interest debt first, such as credit card balances and payday loans. By tackling these debts aggressively, individuals can minimize the amount paid in interest over time and accelerate their journey towards financial freedom.

3. Debt Snowball or Debt Avalanche: Two popular methods for debt reduction are the debt snowball and debt avalanche approaches. With the debt snowball method, individuals prioritize paying off

the smallest debt first, while with the debt avalanche method, they prioritize debts with the highest interest rates. Choose the method that aligns best with your financial goals and preferences.

4. Increase Income: Consider ways to boost income, such as taking on a side hustle, freelancing, or seeking career advancement opportunities. Additional income can be allocated towards debt repayment, accelerating the payoff process.

5. Live Below Your Means: Adopting a frugal lifestyle and living below your means can free up more funds for debt repayment and savings. Cut unnecessary expenses, avoid lifestyle inflation, and prioritize needs over wants.

6. Emergency Fund: Build an emergency fund to cover unexpected expenses and avoid relying on credit cards or loans in times of financial hardship. Aim to save at least three to six months' worth of living expenses in an easily accessible account.

7. Invest for the Future: Once debt is under control, focus on building long-term wealth through investing. Maximize contributions to retirement accounts such as 401(k)s and IRAs, and explore other investment opportunities such as index funds, real estate, and individual stocks.

8. Seek Professional Help if Needed: If managing debt feels overwhelming or if there are complex financial issues to address, consider seeking assistance from a financial advisor or credit counselor. They can provide personalized guidance

and strategies tailored to your specific situation.

By implementing these strategies and maintaining discipline and perseverance, individuals can successfully reduce debt, achieve financial independence, and secure a brighter financial future.

Chapter 6.

Sustainability and Social Impact

- The Environmental Benefits of Frugal Living

Frugal living not only promotes financial well-being but also offers significant environmental benefits, making it a sustainable lifestyle choice with a positive social impact.

1. Reduced Consumption: Frugal living emphasizes mindful consumption and prioritizes needs over wants. By consuming less and avoiding unnecessary

purchases, individuals reduce their overall environmental footprint. This leads to lower levels of resource extraction, manufacturing, and waste generation, ultimately contributing to conservation efforts and mitigating environmental degradation.

2. Minimalism and Decluttering: Frugal living often goes hand in hand with minimalism, encouraging individuals to declutter their lives and simplify their possessions. By owning fewer material possessions, individuals reduce the demand for new products and decrease the amount of waste generated. This minimalist mindset promotes a more sustainable approach to consumption, focusing on quality, durability, and longevity rather than constant accumulation.

3. Energy and Resource Conservation: Frugal living encourages resourcefulness and the efficient use of resources. By adopting practices such as energy conservation, water conservation, and waste reduction, individuals minimize their environmental impact and contribute to global efforts to combat climate change and preserve natural resources. Simple actions such as turning off lights when not in use, using energy-efficient appliances, and repairing items instead of replacing them can significantly reduce energy consumption and promote sustainability.

4. Supporting Sustainable Practices: Frugal living often involves supporting businesses and products that prioritize sustainability and environmental stewardship. By choosing eco-friendly alternatives, such as locally sourced and

organic foods, reusable products, and renewable energy options, individuals can contribute to the growth of sustainable industries and advocate for more environmentally responsible practices within the market.

5. Inspiring Others: By living frugally and embracing sustainability, individuals can inspire others to adopt similar practices and contribute to a broader cultural shift towards mindful consumption and environmental consciousness. Through leading by example and sharing experiences and tips, frugal individuals can empower others to make more sustainable choices and collectively work towards a more sustainable and equitable future for all.

In summary, frugal living offers significant environmental benefits by promoting reduced consumption, minimalism, energy and resource conservation, supporting sustainable practices, and inspiring others to embrace sustainability. By incorporating frugality into their lifestyles, individuals can contribute to positive social and environmental change while also improving their financial well-being.

- Frugality and Ethical Consumption

Frugality and ethical consumption are closely intertwined, as both concepts emphasize mindful decision-making and responsible stewardship of resources. Frugal living involves prioritizing needs over wants and making deliberate choices to optimize spending, while ethical consumption focuses on the social and environmental impacts of purchasing decisions.

1. Conscious Purchasing: Frugal individuals are mindful of where their money goes and seek value in their purchases. Ethical consumers extend this mindset by considering the broader implications of their buying habits, such

as the labor practices, environmental impact, and social responsibility of the companies they support. By aligning frugality with ethical consumption, individuals can make informed choices that prioritize products and brands that uphold ethical standards and promote positive change.

2. Supporting Sustainable Practices: Frugal living encourages resourcefulness and waste reduction, while ethical consumption emphasizes supporting businesses and products that prioritize sustainability. By choosing products with minimal packaging, opting for durable and long-lasting items, and supporting companies with transparent and sustainable supply chains, frugal individuals can reduce their environmental footprint and contribute to a more sustainable economy.

3. Fair Trade and Local Sourcing: Ethical consumption often involves supporting fair trade practices and local businesses to ensure fair wages and working conditions for producers and workers. Frugal individuals can align with these principles by seeking out locally sourced goods and supporting fair trade initiatives, which not only promotes ethical standards but also strengthens local economies and communities.

4. Avoiding Exploitative Industries: Frugality encourages individuals to avoid unnecessary expenditures, including products and services that perpetuate exploitation or harm to people, animals, or the environment. Ethical consumption extends this principle by actively avoiding industries such as fast fashion, factory farming, and environmentally destructive

practices. By boycotting unethical products and advocating for ethical alternatives, frugal individuals can use their purchasing power to drive positive change and hold companies accountable for their actions.

5. Educating and Empowering Others: Frugal individuals can leverage their knowledge and experiences to educate others about the importance of ethical consumption and encourage mindful purchasing habits. By sharing resources, supporting ethical brands, and promoting sustainable alternatives, frugal living can serve as a catalyst for broader social and environmental change, empowering individuals to make a positive impact through their everyday choices.

In essence, frugality and ethical consumption complement each other by promoting mindful spending, supporting sustainable practices, advocating for social responsibility, and empowering individuals to create a more equitable and sustainable world through their purchasing decisions. By embracing both principles, individuals can align their values with their actions and contribute to positive change on both a personal and global scale.

– Giving Back: Incorporating Philanthropy into a Frugal Lifestyle

Incorporating philanthropy into a frugal lifestyle not only allows individuals to make a positive impact on their communities and the world but also aligns with the values of mindful spending and responsible stewardship of resources. Here are some ways to give back while living frugally:

1. Donate Time and Skills: Giving back doesn't always require financial contributions. Individuals can volunteer their time and skills to local charities, nonprofits, or community organizations. Whether it's mentoring youth, offering pro bono services, or participating in

community clean-up events, volunteering allows individuals to make a meaningful difference without spending money.

2. Budget for Charitable Giving: Just as individuals budget for expenses like groceries or entertainment, they can allocate a portion of their income for charitable giving. By setting aside a fixed amount each month or year, individuals can ensure that giving back remains a priority in their financial plan. Even small donations can have a significant impact when given consistently over time.

3. Support Causes You Care About: Frugal living encourages individuals to be intentional with their spending, including charitable donations. Rather than spreading resources thinly across various causes, individuals can focus on supporting a few key organizations or

causes that align with their values and have a meaningful impact. Researching charities, evaluating their effectiveness, and choosing reputable organizations can ensure that donations are used responsibly and make a difference.

4. Utilize Skills and Resources: Frugal individuals can leverage their skills, resources, and networks to support charitable initiatives in creative ways. For example, hosting fundraising events, organizing donation drives, or using social media platforms to raise awareness can amplify the impact of philanthropic efforts without significant financial investment.

5. Promote Giving Cultures: Frugal living fosters a culture of resourcefulness and generosity that can be shared with others. By leading by example and encouraging

friends, family, and colleagues to embrace philanthropy, individuals can inspire others to give back and make a positive impact in their own communities.

6. Explore Matching Programs: Many employers offer matching gift programs where they match employees' charitable contributions up to a certain amount. Frugal individuals can take advantage of these programs to maximize the impact of their donations without increasing their own financial burden.

Incorporating philanthropy into a frugal lifestyle allows individuals to live their values, make a difference in the world, and contribute to the common good without compromising their financial goals. By prioritizing giving back alongside mindful spending and saving, frugal individuals can create a more meaningful and fulfilling life for themselves and others.

The Frugal Mindset

The Frugal Mindset

www.ingramcontent.com/pod-product-compliance
Lightning Source LLC
Chambersburg PA
CBHW071059290526
45795CB00004B/1576